"اتبعوني" قالها مغنيا.

"Follow me!" he sang.

But Mei Ling wanted to finish her drink.
It was cool
It was yummy
And she drank every last drop!

ولكن مى أرادت أن تُنهى مشروبها .
كان باردا .
كان لذيذا .
وشربته حتى آخر قطرة !

وعندما انتهت من الْشرب
كل ما استطاعت أن تقوله هو : "هيك !"

But when she'd finished
All she could say was ... "Hicc!"

ثم جاءَت "هيك" أخرى .
ثم "هيك" أخرى .

And another one came: "Hicc!"
And another: "Hicc!"

HICC!

ليس معقولا !

Oh no!

ضحك بن .
أرادت مي أن تضحك هي الأخرى .
ولكن ما كانت تستطيع أن تقول إلا : "هيك !"

Ben giggled.
Mei Ling wanted to laugh too
But all she could say was... "Hicc!"

قال بن "أنا أعرف ! أنا أعرف !
أمي تقول عليك أن تفعلي
هكذا وتعدّي حتى خمسة . "

"I know, I know!" said Ben.
"My mum says you have to do this...
and count to five."

So they both plugged their noses.
1　2　3　4　5　　and ...
"HICC! Oh no!" said Mei Ling.

وكلاهما سد أنفه وعد

١٢٣٤٥ . . .

"هيك! ليس معقولا!" صاحت مي.

دخلت روبى وقالت :
"أنا أعرف ! أنا أعرف !
يقول أبى عليك أن تفعلى هكذا . . . "

Then Ruby came back in.
"I know, I know!" said Ruby.
"My dad says you have to do this ..."

So everyone tried to look upside down.
1 2 3 4 5   and ...
"HICC! Oh no!"
said Mei Ling.

وحاول كل واحد أن ينظر من أسفل إلى أعلى .
١٢٣٤٥ ...
"هيك ! ليس معقولا !" قالت مى .

Then Leo came back in.
"I know, I know!" said Leo.
"My uncle says you have to do this..."

ثم جاء ليو وقال :
" أنا أعرف أنا أعرف !
يقول عمي عليكِ أن تفعلى هكذا . . . "

وهكذا شرب كل واحد الماء من
الْناحية الأُخرى من كوبه الْبلاستك .
١٢٣٤٥ . . .
"هيك" صاحت مي . "هذا غير معقول . "

So everyone drank water from the other side
of their cups.
1   2   3   4   5   and ...
"HICC! Oh no!" said Mei Ling.

ثم دخل ساهيل وقال :
"أنا أعرف أنا أعرف !
تقول جدتي عليك أن تفعلى هكذا. . . "

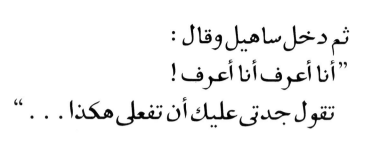

Then Sahil came back in.
"I know, I know!" said Sahil.
"My grandma says you have to do this..."

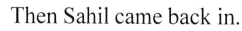

وهكذا كل واحد أخذ يدور ويدور ويدور ويدور:

١ ٢ ٣ ٤ ٥ ...

"هيك. وماذا بعد!" تحيرت مي.

So everyone went spin spin spin.
1   2   3   4   5   and ...
"HICC! Oh no!" said Mei Ling.

ثم دخلت صوفى وقالت :
"أنا أعرف ، أنا أعرف .
يقول ابن عمى عليك أن تفعلى هكذا . . . "

Then Sophie came back in.
"I know, I know!" said Sophie.
"My cousin says you have to do this..."

وهكذا أخذ كل واحد يحرك رجليه في الهواء.
١ ٢ ٣ ٤ ٥...
"هيك!" قالت مى. "لا فائدة."

So everyone did bicycles in the air.
1 2 3 4 5   and ...
"HICC! Oh no!" said Mei Ling.

وفجأة رأت مى بالونتها وطرأت لها فكرة .
وقالت ببطىء : "أنا أعرف . "
"مى لنج ! " صاح كل أصحابها .

But then she saw her balloon and she had an idea.
"I know," she said slowly.
"Mei Ling!" shouted all her friends.

بُب !

قد انفجرت بالونة مى .

POP!
went Mei Ling's balloon.

"إش!" وأنصت الْجميع ليسمعوا هيك من مى .

"Shhhhh!" Everyone listened carefully for Mei Ling's hiccups.

"هل ذهبت؟" سألت مى بهدوء.

"Gone?" asked Mei Ling very quietly.

قال الْجميع: "ذهبت!"

"Gone!" said everyone.

"اسرعوا!" صاح كل واحد.

"HURRAY!" shouted everyone.

ثم بُب! بُب! بُب! بُب! بُب!.. بُب!

POP! POP! POP! POP! POP! AND ...

"ما هذا؟" سأل المدرس .

"What was that?" asked the teacher.

قال الْجميع : "هيك !"
قالت مى : "لاأصدق !"

"HICC!" said everyone.
"OH NO!" said Mei Ling.

For the children of Harry Roberts Nursery,

D.M.

For all the great children and staff of Soho Parish School,
and for Hilary, my lovely supportive mum, with love,

D.B.

First published 2000 by Mantra Lingua Ltd
Global House, 303 Ballards Lane,
London, N12 8NP, UK
http://www.mantralingua.com

This edition published 2014

Text copyright © 2000 David Mills
Illustration copyright © 2000 Derek Brazell
Dual language text copyright © 2000 Mantra Lingua Ltd
Audio copyright © 2013 Mantra Lingua Ltd

A CIP record of this book is available from the British Library

Printed in Letchworth,UK FP110414PB04145538